This book belongs to…

_____

Illustrated by Frank Endersby

Published in Great Britain by Brimax,
An imprint of Autumn Publishing Group
Appledram Barns, Chichester, PO20 7EQ

Published in the US by Byeway Books Inc,
Lenexa KS 66219 Tel 866.4BYEWAY
www.byewaybooks.com

Words and Pictures

Opposites

BRIMAX

When two people or things are face to face,
they are **opposite** each other.

Susie and Peter sit **opposite** each other at the table.

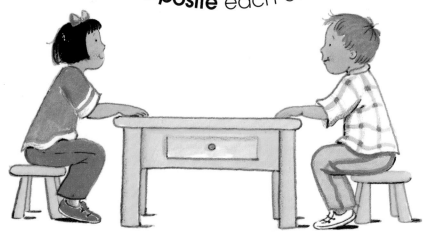

Their house is **opposite** the school.

If something is really different from something else we say that they are **opposites**. Opposites come in twos.
Do you know what these opposites are?

You can have **opposite** sizes...

opposite directions...

opposite sounds...

and **opposite** feelings.

Sizes and shapes

John's father is very **tall**,

but John is very **short**.

This elephant is **big**,

but the mouse is **small**.

Mary walks through a **wide** door.

Paul squeezes through a **narrow** gap.

Mary's sweater has **thick** stripes.

Paul's sweater has **thin** stripes.

Mary's glass is **empty**.

Paul's glass is **full**.

Direction and position

The dog is running **over** the bridge.

The fish are swimming **under** the bridge.

Jenny walks **forwards** to school.

Peter walks **backwards.**

Peter turns **left** to go home, but Jenny turns **right**.

Jenny has lost her toy.

Peter looks **behind** the sofa.

Jenny looks **in front** of the sofa.

Up and down, inside and outside

The plane flies **above** the clouds.

The bird flies **below** the clouds.

Ellen stands on the **high** diving board.

Danny stands on the **low** diving board.

Ellen climbs **up** the stairs and meets Danny coming **down**.

Danny stands on **top** of the hill.

Ellen stands at the **bottom**.

Outside it is snowing.

Inside it is warm and cosy.

Speed and sound, old and new

A cheetah runs **fast**, but a tortoise is **slow**.

A library is very **quiet**,

but a pop concert is very **loud**!

Jane turns the TV **on**…

but her mother wants to turn it **off**.

Jane has an **old** teddy bear.

Bill has a **new** bike.

Weather, temperature and texture

In the summer, the weather is **hot**.

In the winter, the weather is **cold**.

Scamp is getting **wet** in the rain,

but Lulu is **dry** underneath the umbrella.

Sandpaper is very **rough**.

Silk is very **smooth**.

The floor is too **hard** to sleep on.

This bed is nice and **soft**!

Emotions and feelings

There are lots of opposites in the way that we feel.

Wonderful things make
us feel **happy**.

But some things make
us feel **sad**.

When we are happy we **laugh**.

But when we are sad, we sometimes **cry**.

Some things make us feel **calm**.

Other things make us feel **excited**.

When we are
worried, we **frown**.

But nice things make us **smile**.

People

People can be opposites too.

They can be **male** or **female**.

They can be **old** or **young**.

They can be **clean** or **dirty**.

They can be **rich** or **poor**.

They can be **good** or **bad**.

On these two pages, trace a line from each word to its opposite.

smooth   left

sad   in front

low   rough

behind   big

small   happy

right   high

hard

up

over

thin

tall

new

old

thick

soft

under

down

short

Answers:
hard and soft; up and down; over and under; thin and thick; tall and short; new and old.

Look carefully at the pictures and write the missing opposites in the spaces.

1. big and _ _ _ _ _

2. over and _ _ _ _ _

3. top and _ _ _ _ _ _

4. hard and _ _ _ _

5. slow and _ _ _ _

6. wet and _ _ _

Guidance notes

★ This series is designed to encourage children to enjoy learning and to become successful readers at home and at school.

★ Learning is aided by repetition. Looking at the pictures will help children to remember words as well as understand the concept of opposites. The short exercises will help children to learn as they look back and repeat the words and phrases.

★ Stress and worry can affect a child's ability to learn so remember to make reading time fun. Children who struggle to learn at school have proven to benefit from reading sessions with adults at home, in a familiar and supportive environment.

★ As children become more confident, they should be encouraged to read the words for themselves. If a child gets a word wrong, simply correct the word and then move on to another.